CONVERSATIONS FOR
SMART PEOPLE

KOVIE BIAKOLO

CONTENTS

CHAPTER 1.

WHAT HAPPENS WHEN YOU MAKE YOURSELF VULNERABLE

I have always struggled with vulnerability. I like being strong; I've always had to be strong, and I have associated vulnerability with weakness for as long as I can remember. Of course in everyday life, it would be difficult for people to know this. I am seen as someone who is quite open and outgoing, at least to the extent that my demeanor is not mistaken for being a cold, unapproachable bitch. After all, I'm also seen as someone who is known for being blunt; the quintessential, "what you see is what you get" person.

Perhaps it's through writing, perhaps it's through getting older, but ultimately I've realized that I'm a really hard person to get to know. And very few people know even the half of it. I'm guarded and I don't break easily; no matter how close I am to people, I know that most of them are still kept at a distance that is comfortable, a distance that won't leave me exposed. I do not like to be vulnerable.

There is no area that this is true more than the intimacy of romantic relationships. Yes, I play it off as being awkward, and I am. And I play it off as being disinterested in the people who courageously approach me, and maybe that is true too. But when it's all said and done, I am afraid of being vulnerable with people in that way. I like to feel in control of situations, I like to feel that I am always secure and vulnerability gets in the way of that.

When you're vulnerable, your heart is wide open, you put your trust in somebody in the form of giving them the most precious thing you have – your heart. When you're vulnerable you leave yourself available to be hurt and people hurt people. So I guess somewhere along the way, whether I realized it or not, I made the decision that vulnerability was not for me. I told myself that to be vulnerable would mean to give up my strength and I did not want to give it up. My construction of strength almost defined me.

But do you know what happens when you tell yourself that strength opposes vulnerability? I can tell you: Not a whole not, at least not when it comes to pursuing love. Who wants to be with someone that doesn't think they need anyone? And In my attempt to not be vulnerable, I have ultimately been motivated by fear. I have lived in the fear of rejection and the fear of failing in love and I have told myself that it's meant to be this way, at least till now. But the truth is I don't want to be alone. I know I'll be fine and life will go on and other people do just fine with it, but I don't want to choose it if I don't have to.

Lately I've been seeing the error in my thinking. I thought that vulnerability was the weaker position when it comes to love. But I'm realizing that the irony of vulnerability in love and in the pursuit of love is that you actually take the stronger position. When you put your heart on the line, when you give it to somebody and you tell them that it's theirs to keep or break, when you expose who you are and all you are to somebody – that is one of the truest and best strength that there is.

Vulnerability won't be easy, it might be one of the hardest that I'm ever going to attempt. And it might go horribly wrong – I might get broken or damaged like so many others. But I'm not sure this unspoiled heart of mine is any better off. Loving anything and anyone ultimately comes with hurt and my attempt to not let people get close enough to hurt me has left me with a different kind of pain, a different kind of weakness – the weakness of regret and wonder. I think if I am to be truly strong, I think if any of us are, we have to be willing to expose ourselves and put ourselves through the greatest risk of all – which is love.

And in the words of C.S. Lewis, to love is to be vulnerable.

CHAPTER 2.

10 REASONS BEING INTELLIGENT IS DIFFICULT

1. You will be misunderstood a lot. Whether it's the inability to communicate your thoughts in a way that is easily received, or that your articulations are just flat-out cryptic in nature; many times people will just not understand what you're saying. "Never mind" is a phrase that you will use way too often.
2. You'll likely always be frustrated about something. You don't get to go through life apathetically. There is always something wrong – something to be fixed; something to change. But chances are, you can't change it by yourself. So you think about these things a lot. Sometimes you'll tell others about these things too. But it only leads to (1) so you start keeping many things to yourself.
3. Happiness will be a lot harder. Likely because of (2). It will be an everyday struggle to not

want to just give up on humanity and live in a cave by yourself. You don't seem to fit in the world so easily, and you certainly can't fake it as much as everyone else.

4. You'll have anti-social quirks or tendencies. Whether it's talking to yourself in public or having a leg shake when you're deeply focused on something; certain habits or traits will likely cause people to think you're weird. And not in a good/fun/endearing way.

5. Everyone will remember all the times that you get something wrong, and they will never let you forget it! People might even be looking for loopholes and failures in your conversations. When they find them, you shall be berated gleefully. And lo, and behold when they don't find them, you will be labeled a "know-it-all."

6. You'll be hard on yourself when you don't "get things." After all, you're intelligent; understanding things and being imaginative or creative or critical is not "supposed" to be difficult. But no matter how smart you are, there will be things that you don't get. And they will keep you up and night and cause you to believe that you're losing your brainpower.

7. Few will get your sense of humor. Or you'll be so funny that people will inevitably miss the hidden sentiments in your humor. Both will make you weep for humanity.

8. You'll always feel like you're supposed to do great things and feel worthless when you don't. Intelligent people can be successful people but not always; maybe not even often. Sometimes they just don't have the motivation. Many times, the pressure is just too much to bear and you'd just rather lie in bed all day and think about things – imaginative, cryptic things.

9. Because intelligent people aren't always successful people, (and even when they are) you might be subordinate to people whose intellect is well, in need of development. And whether it's in formal institutions or everyday interactions, you will be both humble, as well as saddened that this is your reality till the day that you die.

10. It's a lose-lose situation in terms of your identity. You can't call yourself intelligent without being seen as an arrogant prick. But you also can't also call yourself otherwise, without everyone seeing you as pretentious. And half the time, you're not even defining yourself by your intelligence, other people are. But the minute you take the time to address it, you're pompous. You're silent? You're summoned to speak. You talk? You're being smug. Nope, you can't win. Ever. Which is sad because being smart is supposed to be

fun; but really, it just ends up feeling like a lot of boring and painful work.

CHAPTER 3.

THE ONE WHO CARES LESS

I've often heard that people only start wanting you when they think that you don't want them. It's true; I've lived by it. Whether its business or friendships or especially romantic relationships, the person who cares less always seems to be the person who has the most power. At least that's what it might feel like for the person that cares more. But I question whether this is true or not.

I have been called the, "queen of not giving a shit." One of my many talents is that I am really good at both not actually caring, as well as acting like I don't care. Just yesterday, some girlfriends and I were talking about boys and I quoted Almost Famous as my romance mantra, "If you never take it seriously, you never get hurt." And it wouldn't be the first time I've ultimately come off as cynical about relationships. People think it stems from really not caring; on the contrary, it stems from the fear of caring too much.

I know how to be the person who doesn't text back, who doesn't call back, who waits for the guy to make the first move, and who acts like I couldn't care less whether he does or he doesn't. Being this person comes natural to me because I have convinced myself that being the other person comes with too much potential damage. And I do think to an extent it does. I may never have truly had my heart broken, but I've known people who have; I've been there for them. And that shit isn't fun. It's depressing and devastating and oftentimes a really long journey to returning to being okay.

But the thing is I think people who put themselves out there; people who let you know they care a lot – I think that they have the right idea. I think the human heart especially when it's young, is really resilient. I think that the journey to being okay when one's heart has been broken is a journey that is usually worth facing even when love hasn't done what you wanted. But when you're the one who cares less, who apparently doesn't care at all, you'll go never go on this journey because you'll convince yourself that you don't need to. You convince yourself that you're fine even when you're not.

What people don't seem to realize about the person who cares less or acts like they care less is that they're usually the one who ends up being hurt the most. It is human to want love and to want to be taken care of and to want to take care of someone else. To deny that, is simply to deny one's humanity. Being the "queen of not giving a shit" doesn't make one healthier or stronger or wiser or cooler or even happier. It just makes you feel less human. It makes you feel, less and less.

When it's all said and done, even people who are perfectly lonely and perfectly alone – still need their person. Whether it's a romantic partner, a good friend, a loyal family member – everybody needs a person. And the truth is if you act like you don't care enough, people will eventually start to believe you. So if you feel like you care too much or feel too much or love too much, remember that the alternative is worse. We should all try to seek balance because virtue is that middle ground between any two extremes. But when it comes to love, I don't know if there is such a thing as loving too much or showing that you love too much. And if there is, I think it's commendable; not something to be ashamed of. Because if you don't tell people and show people that you do care, that you do have feelings for them, that you do love them, how the hell are they supposed to know?

So I suppose you can go through life thinking that eventually someone will break down all the walls that you've put up, because you don't want anyone to know how much you can care; how much you can love. But life is short and people are busy. And maybe when the right person comes along, maybe they'll see right through you. Maybe. But if you keep telling yourself that you don't care, maybe you'll also start believing it and you won't even be able to see your person when you find them. So get out while you can and start giving a shit; and if your heart breaks, let it break. Because it'll be okay. You will be okay.

CHAPTER 4.

CONFESSIONS OF AN IMPERFECT CHRISTIAN

What a corny title, isn't it? And yet it is one of the truest phrases I can use to describe myself – an imperfect Christian. But what does that even mean? Christianity is plagued with all sorts of identities and challenges and sometimes resistance, that ultimately calling yourself an imperfect Christian, is from the outset, recognizing that you are an imperfect person.

On the one hand, Christians ought to seek perfection. That is a direct request from Jesus who says, "Be perfect as your Father in heaven is perfect." On the other hand, in my Catholic upbringing, the fact that we are all sinners, the Proverbs quote, "the just man sins seven times a day," and the need for forgiveness and reconciliation, was and is always emphasized. I suppose I was lucky in that respect; my upbringing kept from thinking that I am "holy enough." Oh that word, *holy*. It's said with either a lot of apprehension or a lot of contempt in everyday conversation. It's a word many Christians would rather keep in-group, almost as much as that other word. You know the one – *sin*.

Sin, for all intents and purposes, is an offense against God. And in many traditions, therefore, also an offense against other fellow human beings. It comes in many shapes and sizes; it's active, it's passive, it's overt, it's covert, and if one's conscience is formed in a particular way, and if one is indeed an imperfect Christian, it is always troubling. I am a sinner, and I have no qualms about admitting that. I feel more comfortable around other people who do too; I feel uncomfortable when one claims otherwise.

Of course that is not all I am. Even within this imperfect Christian identity of mine, I believe that I still do some good things; some *godly* things. And I find that recognizing that I am not *just* a sinner is as important as recognizing that I am. You see, I think people forget that we all have multidimensionality to whoever we are, in any and all of our identities. But most of all I think the Christian identity is always a multidimensional one when we consider all the theologies.

The reality is the Jesus who said, "love thy enemy," is the same one who said, "I came not to bring peace but to bring a sword." The same Man who said, "He who is without sin, cast the first stone," is also the Man who took out a whip to flog people who were selling in the temple. This is to tell me that Jesus, who I believe is perfect, is ultimately a multidimensional person, who both forgave sinners, demanded difficult love and sacrifice, and yet embodied righteous anger, and an unfailing steadfastness to the Truth.

If Christianity is to mean anything at all, it means to love Jesus in all His faces. We love the Jesus that was hung on the cross, and we love the Jesus that wears the crown. And somehow, amidst the imperfections of one's life, you find a way to reconcile your *sinfulness* with your *godliness*. Somehow, you find a way to live in an identity, in a body, in a soul, that is always struggling between good and evil, of which the answers are not always as clear as day and night. It requires reflection, prudence, and humility, and above all, an attitude that ultimately one is a mere creature who cannot claim to *completely* know the mind of God.

Of the many things I ask of God, forgiveness is always somewhere hovering at the top. Or at least, I try to remember this. What else can you do when you're imperfect? So perhaps not only do I need forgiveness from God but from my fellow human beings who must put up with my imperfections, who sometimes love me deeply in spite of them. And in the end, must I not do the same to them?

Now love is a complicated matter when you are a Christian because just as God loves all but does not deem all things one does "worth loving." In the same way, I think one can love all or at least try to, – even one's self – while recognizing the need to change, the need to not be so comfortable with one's imperfections. My favorite phrase on love that I heard at a conference once was, "Love without truth is abandonment, truth without love is cruelty."

The truth is the Gospel – the good news – the reason we believe in Jesus, the truth that Jesus came to bring, is a difficult one. And if you consider one's imperfections, it almost seems impossible to reach. Yet I believe as I have been told, that the good news is *always* good, even when it is difficult. One of my favorite phrases of St. Augustine is, "If you believe what you like in the Gospel, and reject what you don't like, it is not the Gospel you believe, but yourself." Sometimes I think our imperfections get in the way of this. But mostly, I think our lack of recognition of the complexity of Christianity and Jesus himself, makes us get in our own way.

It would do us good then, to remember the words of another saint, St. Francis of Assisi, who said, "The Gospel should always be preached, if necessary by words." And somehow, in our imperfections, I think we can still find a way to do good, to say and do what is right, and to live *rightly*. Knowing that virtue is always somewhere in the middle, the big questions don't have easy answers, and humility is necessary in faith, but so is courage. And love – difficult, complicated love – for our fellow human beings above all, can perhaps offer at least some retribution, for all our imperfections.

CHAPTER 5.

STOP BEING YOURSELF

"Be yourself," people say to people. "Live your truth," is another one of my favorites. You know what I say? I say this can be some very bad advice. What is a self? A self is the core of a person. A self is how we distinguish ourselves from other people. But selves aren't made in vacuums. Selves are the consequences of our biology that has been passed on to us from our natural parents. Selves are the result of our environment because we grew up in a certain place at a certain time with a certain of group of people. What we include in our construction of self is indeed socially constructed – both biologically and environmentally. But perhaps most importantly, a self is also a matter of the individual choices that we make.

Language is a very important concept. We don't often pay attention to how we say things and what me mean when we say them in our everyday vernacular. I have often told this story that in my native Nigerian language, Urhobo, there is no word that allows an older person to greet a younger person first; a younger person always greets an older person first. The greeting is, "Migwo" which translates directly in English as, "I am on my knees." An older person responds by saying, "Get up." This interaction is telling of the culture in which respect towards the elderly is emphasized greatly. In language, we find culture and power structures and values of people. I tell this story because it is a foundation for my beliefs as to why "Be yourself" can be useless and even destructive as a way of thinking.

When we tell people to be themselves or live their truths or things of that nature, it seems to me that we are releasing them from a power to make a choice about who they want to be. And dare I say, perhaps who they ought to be. The essence of the notion to be one's self insinuates that there is a self that we have hidden in some magical place where we have a key; and should we decide to, we can use this key to open up the door to this magical place, and voilà our self will be found there. The notion that we should simply live according to what we think are our feelings in the moment, and that this is equivalent to some kind of relative truth that encompasses who we are is not without consequences. Of course we qualify potential consequences to the notion by adjusting for not hurting other people. But even beyond the extremes of potentially telling some people to be themself, there is the negative result of being unaware of our freedom to not just be who we are.

I think the problem with this way of thinking –"be yourself" – is that we make other people and other things responsible for who we are rather than ourselves. I think rendering people to just being themselves is the equivalent of telling them to be nothing other than the sum-total of all the social constructs and popular devices that determine their identity; their self. Telling people to just do what they feel in the moment leaves nothing more than a self that is unprincipled, shaky, and enslaved to one's feelings. And I don't know about you but sometimes my feelings are way, way, off. Sometimes feelings are the last things we should adhere to because what we want and what is good and right and best for us, isn't always the same thing.

Maybe "being who you are" isn't necessarily a bad thing. But it's not necessarily a good thing either. Who we are is terrifying complicated and the sum of so many things; yet at the same time I think many of us know that we can be very simple creatures. I just think that more often than not, when we are telling other people to be who they are, we are failing to recognize that there is choice in who that person can be. And that sometimes it is in our best interests to sacrifice what we want for the choice of what is best. And it is not always because who we are is not good enough. But because by being who we are, we can be selling ourselves short and keeping ourselves from being more, being different, being greater. Being who we are can keep us from being who we can become.

CHAPTER 6.

HOW TO BE A B*TCH

Fail to smile every moment you are in public or around other people, because the first sure sign that a woman is a bitch is any expression that does not indicate happiness.

Be assertive when you talk to people especially when you're standing up for yourself after you've felt insulted or disrespected.

Be genuinely competitive in anything and you will not only be seen as a bitch who is too concerned with winning, you'll also be seen as "manly" because only men compete, women are supposed to collaborate.

Be well-dressed. Bitches are always well-dressed because they are obviously trying to prove that they're better than everyone else.

Be thin. If you're going to be a bitch, you need to have the sort of figure that makes people think you're self-absorbed probably because you work out and try to eat healthy.

Be fat. If you're fat, you're revealing that you clearly don't take care of yourself enough which makes you a burdensome bitch.

Be neither fat nor thin. People will assume that you're a bitch because you're not picking sides, like what is wrong with you? You're making it difficult for people to classify you and that makes you a bitch.

When a guy hits on you at a bar, tell him directly but not unkindly, that you're not interested. You're still a bitch, you rejected a nice guy who hit on you at a bar. What makes you think you have the right?

Swear. Swearing is very unpleasant and un-lady like and bitches aren't ladies as we all know.

Show any kind of annoyance or anger or frustration with life and you have probably ruined someone's entire existence with that display. You're not human, you're a bitch.

Give yourself a compliment. Congratulations, you're not just a bitch but a narcissistic one at that that.

Disagree with a man about anything.

Be too loud.

Be too quiet.

Be too much of something and not enough of something else.

Whatever you do, be a woman who just so happens to not be acting pleasantly enough to please the people around you.

CHAPTER 7.

NOT ANOTHER POST ABOUT PRETTY GIRLS

Yes, another post about pretty girls. Before you sigh and cringe and get ready to spew general disdain, I'm not here to humblebrag or tell you about pretty girl syndrome or pretty girl problems. When we talk about the "pretty girl" as a phenomenon, there are some fundamental questions that surround the discussion: What is a pretty girl? Who decides what a pretty girl is? And what are we to do about it?

The discourse of what constitutes a pretty girl is paradoxically both exhausted and insufficient. We all know and we all talk about how privileged certain conceptions of beauty are over others – whiteness is one example, thinness is another example. The media and we, the people, are continuously shaping and re-shaping the constructions to privilege people with certain features and attributes over others. We are all culprits. We don't like to think that we participate in the constructions but because most of us produce and consume the messages around us that create biases of what beauty is and isn't, we are not exempt from prejudices of beauty. We say Gwyneth Paltrow is a pretty girl and so is Cindy Crawford, Demi Moore, Hale Berry, and all the rest. And so they are.

But those are celebrities who are privileged anyway because of their status. But what about us? What about us, the regular people? Based on our prejudiced standards, we call some people beautiful while rendering others average or ugly. Our conceptions are based on the objective standard of what is aesthetically pleasing to the senses as much as it is based on culturally-specific perceptions. But our senses are not objective because from birth we have been exposed to a limited conception of what is beautiful and cultures, of course, are not impartial. Moreover, cultural conceptions are not equally valued in our world – hegemony perpetuates the beauty discourse as it does most things. A pretty girl is who we say a pretty girl is; the majority rules and it is a tyrannous majority.

When I was younger, I was not considered a pretty girl. When you're a dark-skinned Black African female, you do not start off in the world with beauty privilege on your side. It didn't matter that my family told me otherwise, the world told me that I was not, and so I wasn't. It was often a source of confusion and discontent in my childhood – I was everything else but not pretty. There was a transition, however, a sort of ugly-duckling evolution when all of a sudden, I could be considered pretty by that same tyrannous majority. This is not unusual; one's physical features sometimes change in a way that is found to be more appealing by the majority. But perhaps what changed more was my attitude towards myself — I found a voice, no matter how small, that I wouldn't let that tyrannous majority dictate what I saw when I looked in the mirror.

The consequences of being pretty or being considered pretty rather, are not universal because the experiences that led to that label are not universal. If my story is one of the ugly duckling who had to learn how to say, "Thank you" rather than make self-deprecating clarifications when strangers would comment on how I look, that is not a universal experience. I know pretty girls who have always been pretty and for them the incident of a strangers compliment is an every-day occurrence and expectation. Some of these pretty girls still say "Thank you" and some don't care enough about it to explicitly express gratitude. I know pretty girls who expect things for free and will gladly take them because while the majority considers them beautiful, they are sure as hell going to take advantage of it. I know pretty girls who feel embarrassed to let anyone favor them because of their beauty, and I know pretty girls who explicitly refuse anything given to them by virtue of someone thinking they are pretty. I know pretty girls who are very sure, very certain, very accustomed to almost everyone considering them beautiful. But I mostly know pretty girls who aren't so certain of the tyrannous majority's labeling of them and who are still are as insecure as everyone else is, about the way they look.

The label, "pretty girl" and the way we define it is problematic because it is not something that one is necessarily deserving of, because in its current construction, it can seldom ever be earned. And if you have that label, then there are expectations of how one ought to feel about it which are as arbitrary as the standard itself. So being pretty becomes this thing that everyone talks about and some people have it and some people don't but no one really understands exactly what they are referring to or its implications. And the conversation continues to be exhausting and insufficient.

So what do we do with pretty girls and pretty girl labels? I think we realize in the first place that it is somewhat of a myth — not that it is necessarily unreal because it is as real as much as any social construction is real. But that it is not an objective, entire, and complete notion that is verifiable and exists, ipso facto. If a guy wants to buy me a drink because he thinks I'm pretty, I will gratefully accept if I want to talk to the guy anyway. And hopefully there will be other things he finds about me that are attractive other than those biased senses and conceptions he uses. But maybe it'll do anyone who is in this position to remember that for every one of these guys, there is another, even if he's in the minority who will look at you in terms of solely your physical appearance and say, "What's the big deal?" or worse. And if we all remember that, we'll hopefully be humble enough to realize that the world's standards for physical beauty shouldn't ever be the most valuable thing about us. And perhaps if we all did, the pretty girl label, if it ought to exist at all, can finally be something we're all capable of earning because it'll have more to do with who are than what we look like.

CHAPTER 8.

YOUR DREAMS HAVE EXPIRATION DATES

When I was younger, one of the things I wanted to become was a pro athlete, a sprinter, to be exact. It wasn't a far-fetched dream either; I was pretty fast. But I got slower, and I got less motivated, and I had other interests. Sooner or later, it became clear that it wasn't going to happen. My dream of being a sprinter had an expiration date, and expire it did.

I am admittedly one of those painfully hopeful people who believe that you should never give up on something that you really want. I think that far too many people go to the grave with regrets from not pursuing their dreams. It's not that I believe that pursuing dreams will guarantee that they will come to fruition; I don't. I simply believe that that giving your dream everything you've got is the only way to truly live with yourself.

Of course this idea is met with great cynicism.

The messages that we consume often encourage us to quit, to give up; to be "realistic." And many of us fall prey to these messages because chasing dreams often involves suffering and sacrifice. And suffering and sacrifice are not valued experiences, at least not anymore. We value comfort and we value it a lot. Turn on the television, log into Facebook, go for a walk outside, and all the messages are the same: Be as comfortable as possible.

In our naiveté, we mistake comfort for fulfillment and happiness. And in our effort to be as comfortable as possible, we start chipping away at our dreams. We tell ourselves that once we get enough money or enough experience or meet that right person or move to that right place, then and only then, will we give ourselves the chance. We are always looking for the perfect time to pursue our dreams and tomorrow always seems like the perfect time. Because tomorrow never dies. That is of course, until it does.

Look around you and look inside you. How many people do you think are settling? I will tell you: a hell of a lot of people. People are settling every day into okay relationships and okay jobs and an okay life. And do you know why? Because okay is comfortable. Okay pays the bills and gives a warm bed at night and allows one to go out with co-workers on a Friday evening to enjoy happy hour. But do you know what okay is not? Okay isn't thrilling, it isn't passion, it isn't the reason you get up every day; it isn't life-changing or unforgettable. Okay is not the reason you go to bed late and wake up early. Okay is not the reason you risk absolutely everything you've got just for the smallest chance that something absolutely amazing could happen.

You might not achieve what you set out to achieve when you pursue your dreams; there is a very real likelihood it won't happen. But don't you want to give yourself the chance while you can? Because even though you might not want to give up on your dreams, if you put if off long enough, your dreams could give up on you. Because dreams are not perpetual; they are temporary. Like many things in life, they have expiration dates. And when they expire all you might have left is your comfort. But you may find that your comfort will soon start to resemble regret. And as I'm sure you've heard before: regret is eternal.

CHAPTER 9.

FOR THOSE WHO DON'T LOVE LOUDLY

My mother comes off as a quiet lady to those who don't know her. Married to a man – my father – who oozes charisma and charm in any room full of strangers, my mother is most comfortable being one of those people who is "behind the scenes," if you will. She mostly just loathes being the center of attention, I think. Though my dad is a cool and collected man, his love, his affection, his passion is obvious; it's loud. My mother is almost the exact opposite. And as a child, I didn't understand the way she loved was quiet but fierce – like her. But even then I knew she loved me more than she can ever put into words, even though she doesn't love loudly. And little did I know, that though I would take on some of my dad's charisma in rooms full of strangers, I would grow up to love like my mother.

Vulnerability is still a weakness for me but I think I'm getting better at it. Real vulnerability –

not sending texts at midnight to crushes in a half-drunk state. Or Facebook messaging your feelings or whatever infantile substitutes our generation plugs in the name of love and affection. No, I think real vulnerability means there is no room to save face, there is great possibility for hurt, but there is also great possibility and potential for something that could become love, if it isn't already. And some people do this loudly – they emphatically don't subscribe to any of "the rules" or care to be the one "in power," or mind being the one who cares more, and texts first, and all the other insignificant details we've made so grandeur. Yes, some people love loudly and it's perfectly wonderful. But some people don't.

I used to be jealous of people who loved loudly, secretly, but jealous all the same. While a lot of people seemingly envied my detached demeanor, it came, or rather it oftentimes comes, at a heavy price. No one would ever mistake me for someone who cares too much, even when I have; even when I do. Because unlike those who love loudly, I don't wear my emotions on my sleeve. And even as I wrestle with this weakness that is vulnerability, I don't know if I ever will be that person – the one who wears emotions on their sleeve – and I don't think I have to be.

I think the world is big enough for those who love loudly and those who do not, and those somewhere in between. For those who don't love loudly, we give love in the depth of our affection, not in the frequency. Our passion isn't characterized by the volume in our voice when we're fighting or yelling or crying; sometimes we remain silent because that's the only way in the moment we know how to show love. And we don't walk around with emotions on our sleeves not because they don't exist, but because we believe they are sacred enough, not to have to share them with just anyone. But this doesn't mean that our love is any less.

We love just as deeply and powerfully and passionately when we love. I promise you, we do. Sometimes it's a love you'll find in quiet glances and almost unnoticeable acts of love. Sometimes it's a love we can only express with few words, soft words; words that garner their strength from a foundation that is paradoxically both fragile and firm. But mostly it's a love that though is not loud, is always ferocious, ready to bear anything and everything for those who receive it, in a solitude that we offer to share. So never believe that a love that isn't loud, is a love that isn't there. For those who don't love loudly, our love is quiet but fierce. And our love is always real.

CHAPTER 10.

MY HAIR, MY SKIN, MY SOUL

I've always had really thick, kinky black hair. As a child, my family friend – Aunty Ugochi – as I called her, would come over and do my hair regularly. And the whole neighborhood knew I was getting my hair done because I could be heard crying and screaming, almost as badly as a child getting the cane. My mother did not allow me to perm my hair until I was fourteen – and only allowed it once or twice a year until I left home. My pre-teen and teen years often involved the other girls, especially the Black girls questioning me daily, "Why don't you relax your hair?" Memory is fictional of course, so maybe it wasn't daily but it sure feels like the questioning was as frequent as it was taunting.

My college years were filled with weaves and braids and like my mother had taught me, I still only relaxed it once or twice a year. But mostly being on a campus as a foreign African, Black girl,

I got a lot of questions about my hair; everyone always seemed to have an opinion on how they liked it or what I should do with it, or why it was the way it was. These days, I usually keep my hair in a unique combination of "Ghana Braids" and "Senegalese Twists." I've not relaxed it in almost three years and have had nothing to do with a weave in two. It didn't start out as intentional and I have nothing against these styles, I just choose not to do them anymore until further notice, intentionally.

See when you're a little girl, no one tells you that your hair is political. Sure, it's yours but everyone gets a say on how, when, and what about it too, especially when you're Black. Looking back at photos of my parents, despite my mum's soft, flaky hair, she kept it in an afro and a jerry curl. My dad had his in an Afro too. I used to think it was just what everyone did back then; I didn't understand it was a symbol and expression of their politics, and their resistance. After hating my hair for so long, I braid it these days intentionally as an expression of African identity and because I really like braids. No, I am not my hair. But I like what it means to me.

———

I don't remember the first time I realized I was a dark-skinned Black girl, I'm sure it was earlier than I imagine. I do recall a conversation with my dad in the car when I was eight or nine, maybe older. I told him the kids at school always made fun of me because I was dark. He told me that the kids are silly, and that dark-skinned women were always the most beautiful in his eyes. I never really knew for a long time how people saw me and how they saw my dad were different. My dad is lighter-skinned, and his dad was so light-skinned, he was nicknamed, "Oyibo." – a term for "White people." The best-kept secret in global communities of color is the colorism – the extension of racism – that is often perpetuated among us.

There are several incidents from my childhood and teen years which made me feel ugly because of my skin but one in particular always stands out. When I was ten or eleven, I remember this boy calling me "priceless." He was never very bright and what he mean to say was, "worthless." If it hadn't been for very intentional parenting, and conscientious self-reflecting in my adulthood, who knows? I might have continued to feel worthless instead of priceless, as so many dark girls often do.

It's funny because the times I remember feeling pretty as a teen was when I was in Europe or in the United States, among mostly White people. It's funny because you experience racism being Black in the world, and then you further experience colorism from people who share your experiences as Black, but then choose to "other" you because you are "Blacker." And then the people who are often most privileged for their skin – White people – will often turn around and tell you that your dark skin is beautiful, more than people who share a different shade of your color. It's all ironic and messy.

See when you're a little girl, no one tells you that your skin is political. Sure it's yours but it signifies so many things to the world around you. Now at times I am aware of being sexualized for my Blackness, being othered for it by different people; being considered beautiful for a Black girl, being considered beautiful for a dark-skinned Black girl, and not being considered at all. I used to wish for lighter-skin because I thought that's the only way I would be comfortable. I didn't know that kind of comfort had to come from acceptance and appreciation of self – skin and all. No, I am not my skin but I think it's beautiful the way it is, and I like what it means to me.

———

I've always felt like an outsider, an other. If I could describe what feels normal to me – "being foreign" feels normal. Because I'm not just foreign being an African in the United States, I was foreign being Nigerian and having lived outside of there, all but four years. And indeed I am not always African enough for a lot of people, including other Africans, much less Nigerian enough. To a lot of Black Americans, I "act White," or "African Black but without *their* Black experience." To everyone else, I'm just Black, and until they hear me speak or know me and my background, I am treated in specific ways. I think that's why in social situations, I've always tended to attract "others" too, especially those whose identities involve living in multiple cultures in one body.

But then there's the soul. And I love my soul-I think that's why I'll always be religious and spiritual. Because people can mark your body – they can mark your skin, and your hair, and all the other superficial things about you and tell you have to be something; even something you're not. And for some people with specific bodies, while they must go through their lives with the same mundanities as everyone else, there is an added struggle of ensuring one's own humanity. But the soul, the apolitical soul, is a refuge through which you can really see yourself. And through those eyes, you recognize not only the magnificence of the Creator who made you, but the creature who you see in the mirror, and indeed the creatures who are made in the same likeness.

See when you're a little girl, you don't think about your soul very often. Maybe because even then, no one judges you by it. They judge you by everything else. For a long time I wanted to be the best at everything not just because I've always been competitive. But because I convinced myself that if I could be good at school and sports and dancing and singing and all the rest, then maybe people wouldn't notice my hair or my skin; if I could be the best, then maybe I could at least be good enough. I've learned to love my hair and my skin and take care of them because I ought to. But I couldn't have done it, without first healing my soul. And if you let it, the soul will always heal – with love and time.

———

This hair will fall out, this skin will get saggy, this entire body will fail, and any politics associated with it, will eventually cease to matter. My soul however, from what I choose to believe will hopefully live on forever in perfect love. In the meantime, this soul is still what matters most about me. And not just about me, but every *body* that I meet. I struggle to remember that; I guess I'm still working on it. Hopefully I always will.

CHAPTER 11.

26 THINGS THAT HAPPEN WHEN YOU GROW UP IN AN AFRICAN HOUSE

1. Your parents are basically demigods. It doesn't matter if you learned that the sky is blue. If your parents say the sky is orange, the sky is in fact, orange. At least, in their presence.
2. Your parents will seldom ever admit they are wrong. And if and when they do, you will be too stunned to even believe it.
3. Your grandparents are the only people who can put your parents in their place. (And you will enjoy those moments.)
4. Your house is a free-for-all. At some point a relative, twice-removed, will be invited to stay for an extended-period of time.
5. You will likely be raised the old-fashioned way -"you spare the rod, you spoil the child" kind of old-fashioned way. In your adulthood, you'll largely be grateful for it and

you'll always be able to tell the difference between people who were raised the same way and people who were not.

6. God help you if you're living under your parent's roof and you yell at them, slam a door in anger, and/or curse in their presence. Yeah, God help you.

7. The youngest child will be blamed for everything….until he or she is able to talk.

8. The oldest child will be blamed for everything that the younger children do.

9. If you cry while being accused of something, it is assumed that you are guilty.

10. Your parents will call you from upstairs, downstairs, outside, etc., to hand them something that is literally 10 centimeters away from them.

11. You will not leave your parents' home without learning how to cook.

12. Religious attendance and practice is not an option.

13. Everyone who is older than you is your "auntie" or "uncle." Calling them by their first name is basically a crime against humanity.

14. You will probably never meet all of your extended family because there are just so many of them.

15. This one specifically applies to most Nigerians (although I have to hand it to papa and mama Biakolo for not putting this kind

of pressure on us): Doing well in school is not an option and by doing well, parents have expectations that you will be the best at everything. Example: If you get a 98%, they might ask, "What happened to the other 2%?" If you get a B, your parents will likely ask, "The person who got an A, do they have three heads?" Just do well in school.

16. Your friends better greet your parents first when they see them or that friendship is pretty much over. R-E-S-P-E-C-T is H-U-G-E.

17. Sleepovers at friends' houses are mythical tales or basically only happen when your parents have known the family's family since the beginning of time.

18. Another mythical tale – being in a serious relationship with anyone when you're in your teens. And until your parents believe you are of, "courtship age," they will refer to anyone you are dating as, "your friend."

19. You will still be expected to have a traditional engagement/marriage regardless of where the person you're marrying is from. (Have fun explaining the details of that to all your significant others!)

20. Your parents will talk to you in a lot of proverbs and metaphors. For example, when I was 12, I spent half a day trying to figure out what my dad meant when he said, "When

I talk to you and advise you, do I talk with water in my mouth?" I eventually got it.

21. You will have maybe 3 conversations about sex with your parents – one when puberty starts to take its course, the second one when you start secondary school Biology, and the third one when you are about to leave home. The will all surprisingly sound like the Mean Girl's quote, "Don't have sex because you will get pregnant and die!" followed by "Do not bring shame to this family!" Got it parents, I can't start dating until I'm married and I can't have sex until after I've had children.

22. Your siblings will be the first people to bully the crap out of you. Later on, you'll realize that they were preparing you for a big bad world out there.

23. If your entire full name is being called, and your native language is also being spoken, the day shall not pass without tears.

24. Soda in the fridge? Either your parents were in a REALLY good mood or there are visitors coming over.

25. Surprisingly, alcohol is a hit or miss with African parents. It depends on the set that you get. My dad drinks, my mum doesn't (at all). I got to choose. I chose my dad's viewpoint.

26. You won't realize how incredibly hilarious and somewhat bizarre your upbringing was until you reach adulthood. And you'll burst

out into tears of laughter when you're sitting next to an African woman who is telling her child who probably just got a B, "So the person who got an A, do they have three heads?" Hang in there kid, they secretly boast that they have the best children ever, just not to your face.

CHAPTER 12.

THIS IS WHAT IS REALLY WRONG WITH CASUAL SEX

An article titled What's So Bad About Casual Sex? was published on Thought Catalog. And while everyone is free to have an opinion, I have to say sincerely that article was not a reflection of what casual sex does in its entirety to people, and to society. And yes, while we are all informed by our values, there are some observable facts in society. And indeed when creating an argument, that argument must at least reflect observable facts in society, which I do not believe that article did.

I remember reading a book called *The Sexual Revolution* a few years ago that discussed it as a twenty-first century mistake. The book, like it or not, laid down some very serious consequences of this societal sexual revolution – some being higher divorce rates, broken homes, single-family homes, the explosion of sexually transmitted infections, and of course the severe increase in abortions all under the guise of *choice*. Till this day, whenever I think of sex in the context of the larger societal consequences, I find that this book was spot-on.

There was an opening line in *The Telegraph* once that read like this, "Set free sexually, we are everywhere still in chains." I thought it was an interesting commentary on the state of affairs of much of the modern world where people tend to boast freedom when their very constructs of freedom are ill-informed. Nonetheless years later, I think about that line and while it had a different intention for use, I think about it in the freedom and sex conversations, and I disagree with it. I think a lot of people's attitudes towards sex are still in chains because they are enslaved not only by the attitudes that prevail among a certain Western liberal idea of sex and freedom; but in truth, many have not been able to master their desires – which takes not only freedom, but discipline, and above all other things, love of self and love of the other.

Because when you think of another person as simply an object, in which you put your desire for a certain animal satisfaction above their dignity and humanity as a person, you do not respect this person. And I always believe that when you fail to see a person in all their humanity, you lose yours as well. Beyond this certain objectification that takes place in casual sex where both persons objectify each other, there is a treatment of sex like some kind of forced, animal-like exchange. That we have qualities of animals is a fact, but an essence of human beings is that we are not animals.

I do not write very often about my attitude towards sex because I do not wish to enforce attitudes that come from both cultural and religious values on others. Nor do I wish to be a hypocrite because like every other human, I have sexual desires. I often jokingly tell people, that being a Scorpio – known as the most sexual sign – and a practicing Catholic, God was playing a joke on me. But when I do the work of moral discernment, observing society, and analyzing consequences of particular events, I cannot help but find casual sex to be one of the disturbing events of our time. Not because we are the first to engage in it – we most certainly are not, nor will we be the last. But this generation's *casual attitude* to casual sex is frightening.

We could talk about erasure of sex in which the casual attitude would have one believe sex is only physiological. But ultimately this attitude is a scientific, cultural, and individual deception because sex has and will always be beyond physical. It is psychological, emotional, mental, culturally-informed, and arguably, spiritual. When we conceive of sex as something to just do with someone, somewhere, at any point in time that doesn't matter, it does not change the nature of sex. But it does chip away at our humanity and the way we perceive those around us.

Now while I do not believe in any sort of socio-political governing of the sex act because I believe in liberty, and I believe in liberty because I believe in a God who loved us enough to give us choice in this act. But I also know that the best freedom is not doing what you want, simply because you can – it is making the best choice for the greatest good.

The reality is casual sex has made a society of people who are cold and detached in the ugliest way, from their fellow humans. But above all, casual sex has left many with a self-inflicted and socially-supported brokenness that seems natural when left unchallenged. I am an adult, an adult who knows that as much as I want all my individual actions to *only* be individual, the world is not set up that way. So I encourage other adults to observe society and make your own judgments about what casual sex does and does not do – to any of us, and to all of us. Because while the fantasy seems harmless, the reality seems at the very least, objectionable. And quite frankly, just not good enough.

CHAPTER 13.

WHAT EDUCATION SHOULD TEACH US

I grew up in a house of academics – both my parents were university professors with varying degrees of contributions as public intellectuals in their respective fields. In my upbringing, education wasn't something you went to school and "did" for a couple of hours a day – it was and is a part of my identity, it shapes the way I think and feel and believe; education is a vocation.

Growing up in such an environment, the way I perceive education tends to differ from popular notions and messages of what education is, does, or should do for the individual. In the first place, what do we think when we hear, "education?" Many of us envision the process of schooling where we acquire knowledge in the classroom where our ability to retain, reproduce, and sometimes reframe that knowledge is tested. And as we pursue higher levels of the education process, we move up a structural hierarchy where the knowledge acquisition process is more complex, and there is an expectation that beyond reproducing knowledge, we will adopt critical thinking of any acquired knowledge.

This process, filled with instruction, and instructors, tests, and schedules, and deadlines, in a sense prepares us for organizing beyond the education institutions and systems. We have schedules and deadlines once we begin our lives in the so-called "real world." We also have bosses who will have expectations and projects that will entail instructions and deadlines that we are required to meet. In this way, education institutions do prepare us for work. And because of this, many deem that the sole intrinsic value of education is to prepare the individual to be a productive member of society in the workplace.

Yet I find this positioning of education as solely a preparatory period for a working life inadequate. Education should teach us more than the rules and regulations of becoming a productive worker. Education should teach us how to engage in critical thinking and discourse of who we are as individuals and in relation to the community – the local one we find ourselves in, and the world at large. Education should provide us with the framework for how we choose to participate in society beyond the function of being a worker. This participation should extend to how we arrive at our political and religious constructs, how we choose to consume products and services, and how we choose to interact on a daily basis with the world around us.

It is true that Western hegemony has essentially framed the education process, and as a result, it has become an extension of capitalism. And as an extension of capitalism, the process has become a means to a real outcome. In the liberal arts, we are taught that something is real if it is real in its consequences. And the consequences of education can be a job in our chosen field, a promotion, a title, etc. These are all good things and we should be allowed to want them. But if our education endeavors are only for these sole palpable purposes and our acquisition of knowledge doesn't challenge our beliefs and question our realities, then I don't believe we have received an education; we may have received a degree, but not an education.

Education should be an endeavor in which the learner receives knowledge and encounters and experiences a change in how he or she perceives the world. Education should teach us to be more open-minded, in the sense of wanting to understand better those around us who do not share our viewpoints of the world. Education should teach us to be more conscious of how much good we can do, and to feel a responsibility to leave the world a better place than we found it. Education should lead us to seek more than we find, and to be content even when we do not find at all. Education should teach us to treat each other better because we should understand each other better as a consequence of it. Education should teach us all these things and more because the intrinsic value of education is not that it is a means to any one end, but that it is an end in itself.

CHAPTER 14.

TO BE HAPPY OR GREAT? THAT'S THE QUESTION

One of the characters in ABC's *Scandal*, Cyrus, once said in one episode, "Some people are not meant to be happy. They are meant to be great." It's not the first time I had heard something alluding that happiness and greatness are mutually exclusive. Oftentimes, I wonder if it is true. When we think of heroes, creators, legendary people, one can only imagine the amount of personal sacrifice it takes to truly do something extraordinary. And I have often wondered if part of this personal sacrifice is happiness.

I think that people who do the greatest things on earth often have to face the greatest tribulations. The road to greatness seems like a road filled with disappointments and anguish and more failures than victories. And I don't think many people are willing to travel that road. It is understandable; our humanity is often one that seeks pleasure and avoids pain. And greatness, it seems to me, would involve being able to endure great pains. Pains that may leave the human spirit broken, maybe damaged; maybe pains that accept that happiness is not the sole purpose of one's life.

If you contemplate some of the greatest people in history, from artists to writers to acclaimed political leaders, many underwent severe suffering, including mental illnesses that perhaps made experiencing happiness another struggle of its own. But the point is that they still overcame their suffering and maybe gave up personal happiness because of the calling they felt to do something great, something that would forever leave their mark in the history books. The truth is that many have passed through this earth and many will pass, having done great things, but not great enough to be remembered and their names will not be accounted for in the history books.

Sometimes I think that's what I am most afraid of in life – being forgotten at the end of mine. I can without a doubt say that I do believe that I make a difference to some people's lives. But will I ever do something really great? And if I do, what will I have to sacrifice? As someone who values both happiness and greatness, I am often plagued with the thought that I would have to ultimately sacrifice personal happiness like many have. And when it's all said and done, I don't know which is better. If you had a choice between happiness and greatness, and it was mutually exclusive, what would you choose?

My dad told me something very important when I was young. He said, "Always be happy, no matter what. And if you want to be happy, here's how: be happy." But he also taught me something I've never been able to shake off given our perspective as people of faith. He said, "Remember that on this earth, we cannot be completely happy. Only in heaven, do we experience total happiness." It would seem like a contradictory message but I understand that he always wanted us to be as happy as possible while keeping in mind that this earth is not a place to look for total fulfillment or happiness.

Sometimes I wonder about my dad too. He is a brilliant man, he is still the most brilliant man I know and I don't say that just because he's my dad. Anyone who has a conversation with him knows that he is a man of great intellect. And sometimes I wonder if he chose happiness and a simple life over greatness. And when I think about him, I wonder how many of us make that decision.

My mum, however, who is simply the best human being I know on this planet has always encouraged me to be great. Like many parents, I think she already believes I am. One time during a difficult period in my life, she told me, "There is no path to greatness without great suffering. You must be willing to endure this and more if you're going to do anything you're destined to do." I don't know if I'll ever be great, like George Orwell great or Maya Angelou great or Stuart Hall great, but it sure as hell has been wonderful to have people around me who think I could be.

Still, I don't know what to make of this choice that maybe we all have to make between greatness and happiness; choices that we aren't aware that we make every day. But I do know, for right now, if there are odds I would like to defy, it is to be both happy and great. Maybe both words need to be redefined and maybe they needn't be so mutually exclusive. Maybe if we believe that we are doing exactly what we are meant to be doing in our time on earth, that's how we achieve both happiness and greatness. Maybe you and I, through our sufferings and pains on this earth, and despite them all, and through them all, and whether one person or one billion people remember us at the end of our lives, can lead a life that is both happy and great.

CHAPTER 15.

THINGS YOU HAVE TO LEARN ON YOUR OWN

You have to learn to be strong. Strength is something that people often see as keeping one's self together at all times – never falling and never failing. The truth is the strongest people fall a lot and they fail a lot, but they always endure. Strength is gained from trying, it is gained from participating fully in life; it is gained from facing your fears and from persevering, and picking yourself up after you've fallen greatly. No two people have the same strength because no two people have the same experience. We all have our limits but our greatest strength is discovered when those limits are tried and tested. But you have to learn strength on your own.

You have to learn to be happy. Happiness is not something you can buy or earn, it is something you are and have; it is a state of mind. Sometimes people believe if only they'd get a certain job or move to a certain place or get to be with a certain person, they'll be happy. But it doesn't work like that. Happiness is something that you choose despite all the difficulties that you face. And even in the midst of life's painful events, it is a choice that you can make. Happiness isn't delusional or pretentious and it does not ignore suffering, but it is the choice to be grateful and count one's blessings in spite of suffering. But you have to learn to be happy on your own.

You have to learn to forgive. Forgiveness is one of the most difficult lessons because being hurt is part of the nature of existing. The most difficult people to forgive are the people who are close to us; the people who we love the most. It makes sense of course, those who know what make us most vulnerable have the power to hurt us greatly. And in their human imperfection, they inevitably will. But forgiveness sets you free because hardheartedness cripples you; you are the one who doesn't feel free when you don't forgive. And as much as forgiveness is also for the one who errs, it is more for the one who is wronged. But you have to learn to forgive on your own.

You have to learn to love yourself. Loving yourself is an enigma because on one hand, there are many ways in which you and I are great – there are truly things about us that are wonderful and inspiring. But we also have shortcomings and these shortcomings cause us to question our self-worth and whether who we are is enough for others; whether who we are is enough for ourselves. When you love yourself, you accept your good with your bad and you realize no matter how imperfect you are, your beauty is greater than your imperfections. But you have to learn to love yourself on your own.

I would like to learn all these things to perfection, and I would like to teach them to others especially those who need it the most. But I have found my practice of these things imperfect, and my teaching futile, and I have found myself to be a hypocrite. I am not always as strong as I should be, or happy, or forgiving, and I do not always love myself. So perhaps the most important lesson I have learned is that all of these things that I have to learn on my own are things I'll spend my entire lifetime learning.

CHAPTER 16.

WHY I HAVE FAITH

"Now faith is being sure of what we hope for and certain of what we do not see." –Hebrews 11:1

We all have faith in something – whether it's God, science, institutions, ideologies, and/or our own conceptions of the world, we have faith. Faith is often seen as something in the religious domain and it has been so traditionally. I identify with this domain as a person of faith. And being a person of faith, I often find that people believe that faith is concrete and secure and straightforward. But in my experience, it doesn't work like that.

Faith is hard work, as my mother would say. Most people don't wake up and suddenly have it although I suppose that is possible through divine intervention. Faith, however, is a practice and a habit like many things one can embody. Faith is also having to place your trust in the knowledge that something much bigger than you plays a role in your destiny. Faith is an admittance that neither you nor any other human being or entity is completely in control of all the things that go on around you.

Yet I also grew up with the notion that, "God helps those who help themselves." It is for this reason that faith is not just a theoretical, "pie in the sky" feeling. When you have faith, you also have to act; sometimes you even have to act in darkness. When I say darkness I am trying to convey that you may not be quite sure where the action you're taking will lead. But you have a belief that you're being called to act and that you will be led in the right direction.

Faith can be disappointing, at least in the heart of difficulties and uncertainties. If you believe nothing else about faith, believe that it is the hardest thing to hold onto when you need it the most. Paradoxically, as it's been said, faith isn't faith until it's all you're holding onto. And sometimes, you'll even think all is lost. You'll think that you have failed and whatever battle you were fighting has come to an end; you'll think that you have been defeated. You'll think that your faith has failed you.

I can't speak for anyone else but if there's anything I know at all, it's that my faith has never failed me. In the scorecard of life, I may have lost more than I've won in all the things that I've attempted. But I have always felt like a victor when challenges have come to pass. Because even when I have lost something I worked hard for, and suffered though, and believed in my heart of hearts that I would get, I have found that what was prepared for me was something much greater than I could have imagined. Faith has allowed me to see things clearly.

I can't tell you what to believe or who is right and wrong. That is not even my aim. Faith is a personal journey and in it, you are given choices about what you believe. But my faith, though personal, has made me realize that no one is meant to suffer alone and face challenges alone. Indeed, no matter what I've faced or what those close to me have faced; in my imperfect understanding and fragile faith, I have found that somehow, someway, God has managed to be exactly and perfectly on time. That is my story of faith thus far. The struggle is to remember this the next time I face another struggle, and to never lose faith.

CHAPTER 17.

A CHEAT SHEET FOR WINNING YOUR LIFE IN YOUR 20S

I've always had close friends who are significantly older than me. One awesome advantage to this is they generally treat me to lunch when we go out. (There is such a thing as a free lunch! In your face, Milton Friedman. Okay, obviously the lunch isn't technically free but it's free for me and that's what counts.) Anyway, the other great advantage is I get a lot of tips and tidbits of good advice about how to enjoy my twenties and be independent and all that good stuff. Honestly, I feel like I've been in my twenties a really long time even though I'm not even at the half way point yet. But when you move across the world at seventeen by yourself, you grow up really fast. So, I've taken it upon myself to curate a cheat sheet for how to win at life. Of course, I am still working on almost all of these.

1. **Education**

- Your undergraduate degree is only as relevant as you want it to be. If it gets you the job of your dream — great! If not, show how your entire college experience makes you valuable in the "real world."

- If you know you want an advanced degree, get it done early. It gets harder as you get older.

- If you can work for a company that will pay for your advanced degree, do it. It's a small price to pay.

- Institutions are not the only place where you learn. If you can teach yourself a valuable skill through reading and practicing on your own time, do it.

2. **Career**

- Even the shittiest job has something to teach you. Learn it.

- Decide your "why" for working. If you want to make a lot of money, be willing to potentially sacrifice time, effort, and personal satisfaction. If you want to be happy in your chosen field, be willing to sacrifice money. The two, however, needn't be mutually exclusive.

- Have a side hustle. We live in uncertain times

and if you can be in charge of how much you make in one stream of income, you will be better off.

- Never ever stop networking.

- Don't be afraid to try something you never thought you'd do.

- Know more than your resume.

- Never burn bridges no matter how awful your boss and coworkers are.

- Don't become your career.

3. Love – Family and Friends

- Your family probably still knows you the best and are still likely the people who will have your back when shit hits the fan. Appreciate them.

- Realize that your parents really do want what is best for you. Given that they probably have vast years of life experience on you, they're advice is worth at the very least, taking into consideration.

- Your family will disagree with some of your choices. Accept it.

- Your friend group will shrink. Live with it.

- Don't be afraid to break-up with bad friends.

- Never become the sucky friend who is in a relationship and forgets about their friendships.

- Be intentional about the people you want in your life.

- Be the friend you would want to have.

4. **Love – Romance**

- Be in love and happy with who you are, first and foremost.

- You may have feelings for someone but if you know they are bad for you, take to your heels.

- Stop believing that someone is going to change for you.

- Before you move for love, make sure you'll be happy with where you move to too.

- Enjoy the times you're single. You might not always get to be selfish.

- Whether you're single or in a relationship, realize that it is a choice. If you want to make a different choice, recognize the sacrifices that will inevitably need to be made.

- Your heart will likely be broken by someone. No matter who, when, why, and how, never ever let someone else make you bitter.

- Be willing to take the risk of getting rejected for the reward of falling in love.

- Try some form of online dating at least once.

- Ask someone out the old-fashioned way at least once, whether you're a guy or girl.

5. **Life & Miscellaneous**

- If you want something, promise yourself that you'll at least try no matter how unworthy or unprepared you think you are.

- Actually learn from your mistakes. If you see a pattern — stop, find the source, make a change.

- Ask for help when you need it. Even from mum and dad. There is no shame in needing help.

- Put yourself in uncomfortable situations, on purpose.

- Don't take advantage of the people who help you by becoming complacent and irresponsible.

- Pay your bills on time.

- Be nice to your landlord, your credit card company, customer service, etc. They can be understanding if things get tough.

- Attempt to budget. Keep attempting.

- Save what you can. Even if it's $5 a week. Do it.

- Whenever you can, travel. Even if it's within your borders.

- Sales are good. Free is still better and nothing to be ashamed of.

- Don't compare yourself to your peers.

- Recognize that no one expects you to have it all figured out. But don't be a hot mess ALL the time either.

- Have fun or when you hit 30, you'll wish you had fun.

- Work hard. Play maybe as hard, but not harder. Sleep.

- For every current big, awful, problem (see: problem that is not that big in the grand scheme of life), remember the last big, awful problem that you had, and that you came through it.

- Be grateful for at least one thing every day.

- Always believe that whatever is meant to be, will happen.

- Yeah, so have fun with this. I said it was a cheat sheet, I didn't say it'd be a short one!

CHAPTER 18.

DECONSTRUCTING WHITENESS AND WHITE PRIVILEGE

I've been trying to write an article solely focused on White Privilege for months. There are a plethora of books and articles by people much more qualified than me to talk about these matters. There are many scholars dedicated to this subject matter. I am but an apprentice attempting to do so in a somewhat easy –to-read article in the digital space. But race is on the mind of the nation; it always is but evermore so this week. And I believe it is an opportune time to gain greater understanding of race relations and particularly the subject matter of Whiteness and White privilege.

I am a runner and for the past 6-8 weeks, I'd been training for half-marathon season as I call it, when I do longer races. Unfortunately, I've been struggling with some knee and feet injuries. I've had injuries before but nothing that I couldn't shake off quickly. Now I'm questioning whether I should be running these races because of the biomechanics of my body and the recurring injuries. Most of the time, I don't think about my knees or feet. I am aware that they are there but I do not walk around conscious of them. This is the privilege of someone who is able-bodied. Someone who is not able-bodied might think of their body and parts of their body more than someone who isn't. And White privilege, though is intrinsically different, works somewhat of the same way. White people generally don't go through the world thinking about being White. But the reality is non-White people, at least from time to time, do.

Sometimes when I have encountered people who are not able-bodied as myself, I feel a twang of insecurity. I don't want to say the wrong thing or act the wrong way. But an able-body is the privilege that I have been given in a world that assumes able-bodies as a norm. Whiteness, even in a world where non-White persons have larger numbers, is the norm of the societies that most of us live in. And this is especially so in Western civilization; it is especially so in the United States.

That race is socially constructed is a sociological phenomenon. But social constructions are not without real consequences. And a real consequence of Whiteness and White privilege is that persons who are not considered White often have to justify their existence – in whole or in parts – in a way that White people often do not. An easy and not too uncommon example: The way I talk often complicates people's perceptions of me. I have been told many times that, "I speak so well." I consider myself a good orator but I know most of the time, the pseudo compliment is based on the lack of expectation that a person of my skin color and perhaps my national origin can speak the way I do. White people who speak as I do are seldom ever told that they are, "well-spoken." They don't need to be; it is assumed. And that is how privilege works.

Privilege infiltrates all areas of life and this isn't always obvious to persons who experience privilege. There are of course blatant examples of White privilege such as the socio-economic discrepancies between members of different racial groups, which are representative of discrimination histories. Certain groups are born into more wealth which makes it more likely for those groups to maintain better opportunities for education, health, employment, and overall a better quality of life over others. But White privilege is also subtle and murky. It so ingrained into the fabric of much of Western civilization and the hegemony that it has perpetuated for centuries, that changes in law do not necessarily bring about de facto changes in society especially in subtle ways.

I remember once having a cut on my finger and putting a purple plaster on it. An acquaintance who is White commented on my purple plaster, saying she thought it was cool that I went with a fun color rather than a boring nude color like everyone else. Trying not to sound peeved, I explained to her that while I like purple, there are also no "nude" plasters for people of my skin color. I could see she was embarrassed because essentially what I had done is call a privilege out that she wasn't even aware of. She then frankly told me, "I had never even considered it. Ever."

And that's what privilege is – not considering something because you don't have to. When you have White privilege, you don't have to consider many things; when you don't have it, you do. You consider it when you walk into a store and you wonder if the sales people just so happen to be on the same route as you or they are indeed watching you because of the perception they have of people of your skin color. Note that sometimes these sales people need not be White either. You consider it when you're in class and race issues have come up, and perhaps as the sole representative of a particular race in that class, you are essentially expected to speak on behalf of the people of that race. You consider it when you are watching television or reading a book or spending time on the Internet and being told that this is beautiful and that is wonderful; but all those beautiful and wonderful things are mostly represented by only one color of people. And you consider it when you raise the issue of race in any context and are accused of playing a supposed race card and of "making everything about race."

The social reality is that Whiteness and White Privilege perpetuate because of subtleties and invisibilities. For example, pay particular attention to a conversation the next time you can, and notice which races get pointed out and which does not. Another great example some classmates gave earlier this year too was the "Shit People Say" phenomenon. The video that started it all, "Shit Girls Say" didn't need a racial qualifier like most other subsequent videos that parodied what girls of other races said. Even when Whiteness gets a racial qualifier, it is not without privilege. Consider the term, "White trash" and how it has to be linguistically specified that this person is "White" but also "trash." Other races that may fall into similar socioeconomic backgrounds as poor White people don't need the racial linguistic qualification. Language mirrors reality more than most of us are aware of. Even a term that is meant to be a pejorative for a racially privileged group, still ends up exposing privilege.

The purpose of understanding White privilege and Whiteness is not to point fingers or place blame on entire groups. The purpose is to understand how many of us, including those who are disadvantaged by the system are still complicit in that system. The purpose is to be more aware of our thoughts, words, and actions, and how they might contribute to a system that disadvantages entire groups of people. And for what? Because of a shade of color?

I have to go and get my knees checked out tomorrow for one final analysis to see whether I can run this half-marathon on Sunday. I've not been made aware of my privilege of being able-bodied in some time so this is good for me. It's good to be reminded that I didn't do anything to earn this privilege to be seen as healthy and capable by virtue of not having a physical disability. I didn't earn the right to live in a world where being able-bodied is the assumption; the norm. But that doesn't mean I shouldn't be more cognizant of my privilege. It doesn't mean I can't do my best to treat other bodies that are not like mine, as equal and worthy of a good quality of life. In the same way, I hope that White privilege will one day open up the eyes of many – those benefiting and those disadvantaged – to treat people, regardless of their shade of color as being equal and worthy of a good quality of life. And you begin in your own mind, in your own heart, and with your thoughts, words, and actions. Then, you start with your neighbor. Because that, more than any laws that will ever be put forth, is what will change the system.

CHAPTER 19.

WHY EVERY GIRL NEEDS ROLE MODELS WHO LOOK LIKE HER

A few days ago, Ashley Lee wrote a piece, "The Color of Beauty Is Hard To Imagine: Growing Up Black In A White Community." It's a piece that I think many Black females who find themselves assimilated in America's White mainstream culture can identify with. As a Black African, I could still identify with that piece despite having grown up in diverse schools and communities. And after living in the United States for six years, it was very easily relatable. White, Western, and particularly American popular culture and standards are not limited to borders of Western countries; it permeates almost every corner of this earth.

I, however, as an African do not pretend to understand what it is to be American, and especially to be African-American. I engage in race and privilege discourse a lot but I do so mostly with a critical academic lens and a limited personal narrative. I think it would be as aggravating for me as a Black African to purport to completely identify, understand, and experience the Black U.S. American experience, as when non-Black Americans attempt to do so. Still, when I read Ashley's article, I was a little stuck and heartbroken. Not only for her but for the many women and girls like her who have had to go through or continue to go through an experience of thinking that they are not enough in one criteria or another based solely on the color of their skin.

For some reason, the Clark Doll Experiment of 1939 came to my mind when I read the piece. The one where little Black children preferred White dolls to dolls who looked like them; dolls who looked like them – Black dolls – were bad. This experiment has been re-done many times and despite living in (theoretically) less prejudiced times since the first experiment, the results have more or less been maintained. However much change American society has undergone in its race relations, there is still a lot of repression to alleviate. There is still much healing and much more change in thinking, that needs to be done.

After thinking about this experiment, I emailed my Dad and asked him why he bought me Black dolls growing up. He sent me a script of this speech by one of our favorite popular Nigerian authors, Chimamanda Adichie. In the speech she talks about the danger of a single story about any place or people. Additionally my dad wrote, "I wanted you to be able to tell your own story, to be you, and to stay proudly yourself." I am not too embarrassed to admit that I got a little teary-eyed because I became very grateful for my parents. And reminiscing, my parents – both my mum and Dad – despite knowing that I would grow up in a world where I might have to be conscious of my skin color, they wanted me to know that I never had to want to be someone else because of it.

Yet as a child and as a teenager, because of my darker shade of brown, I endured a lot of repugnant remarks. And I think without the deliberate parenting of the two people who raised me – I think it might till this day, have negatively affected how I thought of myself. Because the truth is once I became aware of the standards of beauty as a child; away from the happiness and comfort at home, I did feel ugly because of my skin. I wasn't comfortable in it. I don't recall if I ever wanted to be White but I recall wishing I could be lighter, which would make me closer to being White.

I grew up, however. And from time to time, I would remember being happy as a little kid that I had a doll to play with that represented me. And I grew up thinking about my mother who is without a doubt, my biggest role model and a true classic beauty – both inside and out. I think of how wonderful it is that people think I look like her – a little bit or a lot. And I grew up and looked for images of beautiful women like Iman, like Oluchi Onweagba – women who looked like me but were famous for their beauty. And I grew up and I sought authors like Chimamanda Adichie who encouraged me, just like my dad always had – to tell my own story; to tell the world my own story.

When you're a girl, you are born into a world that judges you by your physical attributes, which are mostly based on arbitrary standards. I suppose some people would say I have nothing to complain about now – my physical attributes are appealing to some, to many, "despite" being Black. But I would rather live in a world where race didn't play so much of a role into what one thinks of themselves – in terms of beauty or intelligence or one's capabilities. I would rather we learn to see the different colors of people as beautiful in their own right. But till that day, I urge that every little girl is given role models who look like her. So that even if the world tells her otherwise, she will know that her shade, her color, her story, is absolutely beautiful. Because knowing this can save her; at least, it saved me.

CHAPTER 20.

WHAT I THINK ABOUT LOVE

The first experience of love for most of us is from our parents. I am no different. I always knew that I was loved as a child by the people I call "Mum" and "Dad." I was also brought into the world with three older brothers as siblings. And no doubt, even as a child, I knew that my brothers loved me very much. They always made a fuss over me and they are part of the reason that growing up, I felt very spoiled with love. But I think the first real lesson I learned about how to give love and not just receive love was the day I became a big sister.

Thirteen years later, my favorite memory and the best day of my life is still the day my sister was born. I will never forget the feeling of that moment of looking at her for the first time and that sensation of pure and utter perfect love. It's the only honest love at first sight I have ever experienced. From that day, I think I knew what giving love is supposed to feel like. Because it felt like I would do absolutely anything for her in the world. I was going to love her with all I had and give her everything I had to offer. It was really that simple.

And my sister's love is probably some of the purest I know in the world. Maybe it's because she is young enough, and life hasn't ruined love for her in the way it does for most adults. Even though we are separated by oceans, I know that her love for me is honest, unwavering, and so independent of moods or motives or anything else. I know that I am loved deeply by my parents and brothers and a few very good friends. But there is something about being loved by a child that can teach you that love can be simple and pure and uncomplicated.

I go back and forth between being a cynic about love and a hopeless romantic – an often closeted hopeless romantic, but one nonetheless. When I look around me and I see most of the relationships of my peers, the truth is I do not feel comforted. I see people who are selling themselves short just to have any kind of love. I see people who want to engage in unnecessary fights and quarrels under the guise of passion. I see people who are so dependent on each other for validation and an identity. And I see lust and the fear of being alone and the need to be wanted by anyone, as substitutes for love.

But why does this generation feel the need to

make love so complicated? Is it just limited to this generation? Is love complicated regardless of space and time? I don't know. And maybe this is where my hopeless romantic comes into play. Because I don't need romantic love to be the be-all-end-all of my existence. I just need it to complement who I am and the person I love to be. I don't need love to feel like I've given up on trying and will settle for what's available because I'm exhausted. I need it to feel like we deserve each other because we authentically want each other. And I don't need love to have this ever-burning fire of emotion. I need it to be sincerely passionate but calming and playful, in a world where so many things can stress you out. I don't need love to solely prevent a lifetime of aloneness. I need it to feel like a true friend, a true companion, will care for me simply, purely, and as uncomplicatedly as possible. And I will do the same.

Maybe love is the easy part and everything else is complicated – relationships, marriage, etc. Or maybe it's just people who choose to be complicated and choose to make their love complicated. And as the cynical part of me is trying to die slowly each day, I realize more and more that I just don't want complicated love. It's not that I think love from any person is perfect because it's not; people are not perfect. But it shouldn't feel like the difficult task and burden that I seem to witness. It shouldn't feel like constantly wrestling for a sign of certainty from the other person; anxiously waiting for their phone call, endless tears and never-ending fear of making one minor mistake that could leave you heartbroken. Because this is what I mostly witness from my generation. But I just can't believe that this is it – this can't be it especially when we're so young.

Love is a sacrifice. It's a desire to want to take care of another person. It's putting that person's needs before yours. It's accepting the disappointments and imperfection of that person and dealing with the pains that come with that. But love, especially when you're young should also be fun. You should feel the heat but not feel like you're getting burned. It should be about laughter and it should be light; it should be simple.

And if the other stuff that comes after love is complicated then we learn to deal with it along the way. But if the love is so complicated in the first place, I just don't know if that's a road worth travelling. Maybe I'm wrong and maybe I just have no clue what I'm talking about. Or maybe you and I as *The Perks Of Being A Wallflower* famous quote states, accept the kind of love we think we deserve. Because I think the kind of love that we let in our lives tends to change us; it defines us. And thus we become defined not only by the love that we give, but also by the love that we are willing to receive.

CHAPTER 21.

EVERYTHING IS GOING TO BE ALRIGHT

My grandmother on my mother's side is the only living grandparent I have. She's the only one I've ever really known. We all call her "mama." She has seen more in her lifetime than most people ever will: She has survived a civil war, great poverty for much of her life, a child and grandchild passing on the same day, and much more than she would ever tell. The last time I saw my grandmother when I was visiting Nigeria, she said to me that my brothers and I have to build her a new house before she passes. In literal terms, she meant that she wishes to see my siblings and I succeed even more while she is alive. Somehow in spite of everything, my grandmother is alright.

Both my grandfathers died before I was born – my maternal grandfather saw my mother while she was pregnant with me but he is said to have died of heartbreak. He died soon after he found out his daughter and his grandchild had died – my mother's sister and niece. That was the year I was born. My mother lost three loved ones while she was pregnant with me, and had it not been for a miraculous intervention during my birth, she would have lost me as well. My mother ends every conversation with, "Remain Blessed." Somehow in spite of everything, my mother is alright.

My father used to write against Nigeria's dictatorial governments in the 80s and 90s. He knows what it is to fear for life, to leave a cause behind, to lose everything and have to rebuild. Yet the only time I've ever seen my dad come close to tears was when he lost his mother when I was ten years old. We lived in Botswana at the time and he never got to say goodbye. He had been the one to close his dad's eyes, and I suspect that it's only through prayer that he finds peace in being unable to be there for his mother in her final hours. As he often says, "Life goes on and so must we." My dad is alright.

The summer and fall after college, when I was no longer going to law school was a summer and fall of a lot of tears. I was confused, I was scared, and I was broken to be perfectly honest. And after I ended up working for a startup that eventually failed, I was broken some more. I moved four times last year, and for the most part, I would characterize my life after college up until this year as, "one thing after the other." But I'm alright.

My family, my friends, and my experiences have something in common – we're all, alright. Saying "everything is going to be alright" can be aggravating in the moment, it can be the last thing that any of us really want to hear. In the moments that we hear these words, we're not quite sure that everything is going to be alright. If we're honest, a great part of life is suffering, pain, failing, and uncertainty. It's why we all relate to sad stories easily. And while life is also happy and full of joy and laughter, I think it's important to find peace of mind even when things aren't going well. I think that's one way to have authentic happiness – to find it in authentic pain.

I tell people that they're going to be alright all the time. And I used to say it superfluously; just because it was something to say. But I found those words can be the most meaningful things people say. When I was sixteen one of my last volunteerism activities while living in Botswana was visiting a young girl who was dying of AIDS. I believe we were around the same age and I went with our parish priest to give her Communion and visit with her. I have never seen anyone so weak in my entire life. The next day the priest told me she was dead. I still remember the numbness that overtook my senses. He said, "She's alright, you know? She's finally at peace." I have to believe it.

When I think of that story, and I tell people that everything is going to be alright, I don't tell them that because it's something to say, I say it because I believe it; I have to believe it. People are in pain in so many different ways. And sometimes I am overwhelmed by just how awful this fallen world is; I am overwhelmed by how awful we are to each other. And when we are facing what seems like something greater than what we can handle, we can feel abandoned, helpless, and hopeless. We can forget that what we are facing, in fact – all that we are facing – is ultimately temporary.

Because when I think about the people that have come before me who have faced so much more than I ever will; and even when I think about my very short life story so far, there are just no better words than, "Everything is going to be alright." Because in the end – sometimes quite literally – it is. So if you ever find yourself not knowing what to believe anymore, I hope you'll at least believe that somehow, someway, everything is going to be alright.

ABOUT THE AUTHOR

Kovie Biakolo is a Nigerian transplant to the world who has lived in the States since she was 16 and 3/4 years old. She has a background in digital marketing and multicultural and organizational studies but believes her best knowledge-base comes from failing at many things during her early twenties, which eventually got her into writing. Kovie considers herself a connoisseur of intelligent life topics because she reads a lot and has more degrees than ex-boyfriends.